HOME EDITION
GOSPEL PROJECT
FOR KIDS

The Gospel Project: Home Edition
Grades 3-5 Workbook Semester 2

Workbook Pages to Supplement
The Gospel Project: Home Edition Teacher's Guide Semester 2

No part of this work may be reproduced or transmitted in any form or by any means, electronic or mechanical, including photocopying and recording, or by any information storage or retrieval system, except as may be expressly permitted in writing by the publisher. Requests for permission should be addressed in writing to

LifeWay Press©,
One LifeWay Plaza, Nashville, TN
37234-0172.
ISBN: 978-1-5359-1584-7
Item 005805929
Dewey Decimal Classification Number: 220.07
Subject Heading: BIBLE—STUDY\THEOLOGY—STUDY\GOSPEL—STUDY

Printed in the United States of America
Kids Ministry Publishing
LifeWay Resources
One LifeWay Plaza
Nashville, TN 37234
Nashville, Tennessee 37234-0172

We believe that the Bible has God for its author; salvation for its end; and truth, without any mixture of error, for its matter and that all Scripture is totally true and trustworthy. To review LifeWay's doctrinal guidelines, please visit *www.lifeway.com/doctrinalguideline*. All Scripture quotations are taken from the Christian Standard Bible © Copyright 2017 by Holman Bible Publishers. Used by permission.

CONTENTS

How to Use this Book	3
Joshua and Caleb	4
The Bronze Snake	6
The Promised Land and Jericho	8
Achan's Sin and the Defeat of Ai	10
Joshua's Final Encouragement	12
The First Judges	14
Deborah and Barak	16
Gideon	18
Samson	20
Ruth and Boaz	22
Eli and Boy Samuel	24
Israel Demanded a King	26
God Rejected Saul as King	28
David Was Anointed and Fought Goliath	30
David and Jonathan Became Friends	32
God Made a Covenant with David	34
David Sinned and Was Restored	36
Solomon Asked for Wisdom	38
Wisdom for God's People	40
Solomon Built the Temple	42
Solomon's Sin Divided the Kingdom	44
Job	46
Solomon Thought About Life	48
Praises of God's People	50
Teaching Pictures and Bible Stories	52
The Gospel: God's Plan for Me	64

HOW TO USE THIS BOOK

For Kids

Congratulations! You are about to take an 18-week journey through stories that take us from the time of Joshua to that of Solomon.

You are going to learn that although the Bible has a lot of stories, there is really one big story that is being told of God's plan for people. It shows God's great salvation plan: God created us. We sinned. God promised us a Savior and sent Him—Jesus—for us. Jesus died for us so we might live with God forever. We respond by believing. (See page 64.)

Did you notice that you are part of God's plan? Yes, it's true! Jesus died for you, and you can respond and believe to become part of God's ongoing plan to bring others to know Him. Let's take this journey together!

For Parents

Use these activity pages, Bible stories, and teaching pictures as directed during the 18 weeks of teaching plans in *The Gospel Project: Home Edition Teacher Guide Semester 2* (005793046) or *The Gospel Project: Home Edition Digital Teacher Guide Semester 2* (005806157).

Promised Land Maze

Move through the maze to collect each cluster of grapes. Avoid the people already in the land. No backtracking!

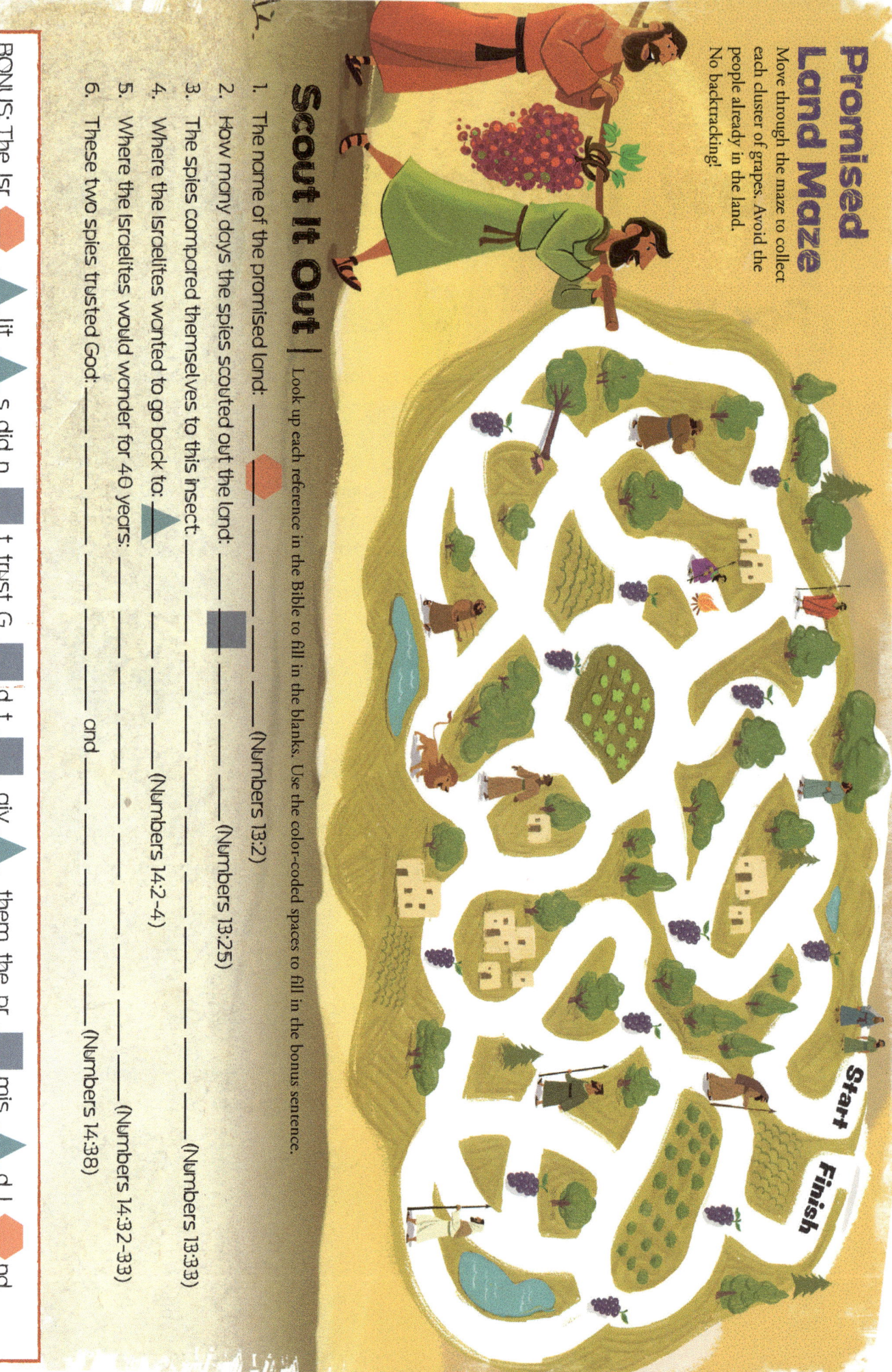

Scout It Out

Look up each reference in the Bible to fill in the blanks. Use the color-coded spaces to fill in the bonus sentence.

1. The name of the promised land: ⬡_____ (Numbers 13:2)
2. How many days the spies scouted out the land: ▪_____ (Numbers 13:25)
3. The spies compared themselves to this insect: _____ (Numbers 13:33)
4. Where the spies wanted to go back to: _____ (Numbers 14:2-4)
5. Where the Israelites would wander for 40 years: _____ (Numbers 14:32-33)
6. These two spies trusted God: _____ and _____ (Numbers 14:38)

BONUS: The Isr⬡__ ▲lit▲s did n▪ __t trust G▪__ d t▲giv▲ them the pr▪mis▲d l⬡nd.

JOSHUA AND CALEB 4

Journal Page

Write about a time you felt weak or afraid. Remember that we can trust God to take care of us. God has the power to make us strong and courageous.

_____
_____
_____
_____
_____
_____
_____
_____
_____
_____
_____
_____
_____

FAMILY DISCUSSION STARTERS

- Do you think it was easy or hard for Joshua and Caleb to take a stand for God? Why?
- What do you have a hard time trusting God with?
- Talk about other times when God has kept His promises.

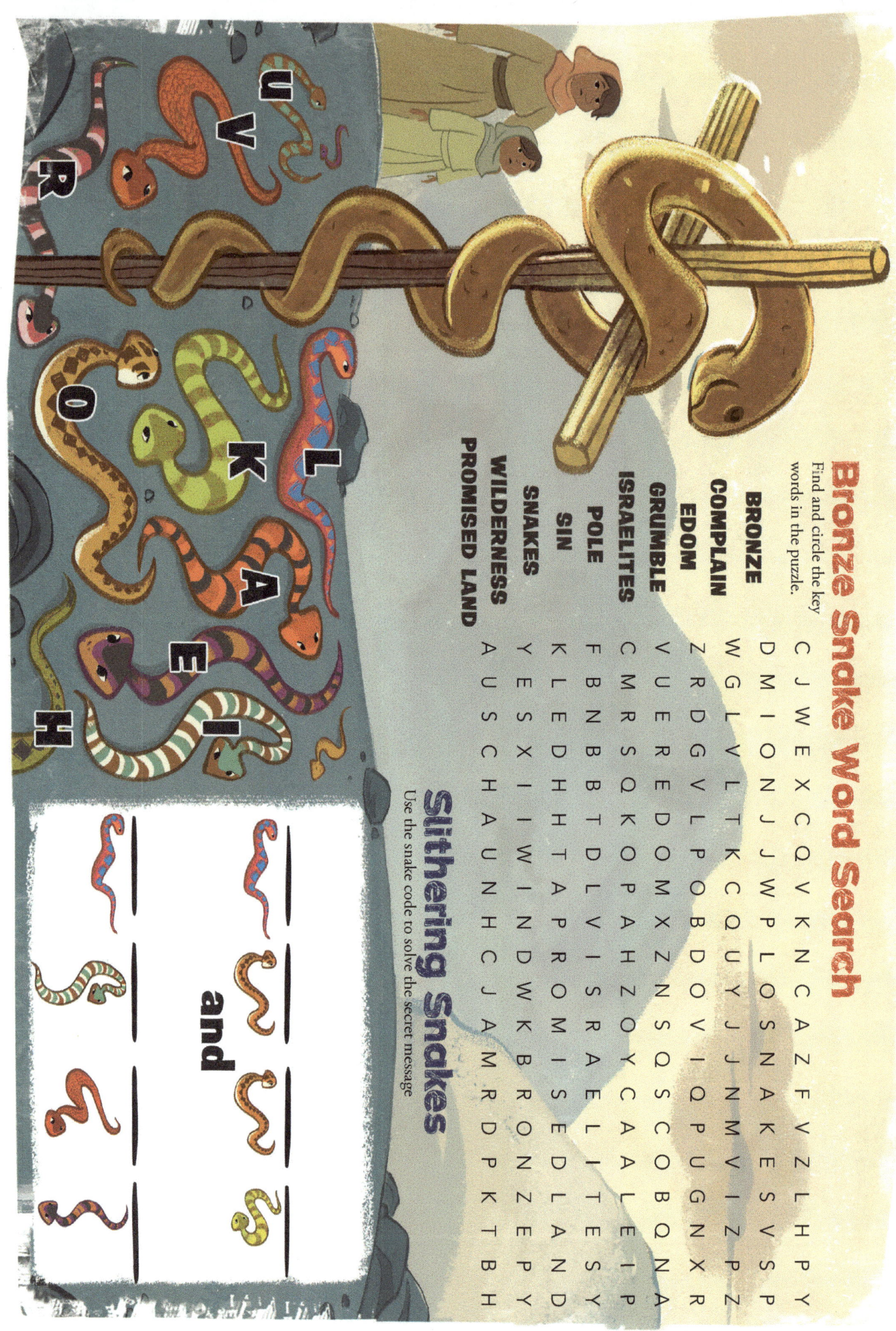

Bronze Snake Word Search

Find and circle the key words in the puzzle.

BRONZE
COMPLAIN
EDOM
GRUMBLE
ISRAELITES
POLE
SIN
SNAKES
WILDERNESS
PROMISED LAND

```
C J W E X C Q V K N C A Z F V Z L H P Y
D M I O N J J W P L O S N A K E S V S P
W G L V L T K C Q U Y J N M V I Z P N Z
Z R D G V L P O B D O V I Q P U G N X R
V U E R E D O M X Z N S Q S C O B Q N A
C M R S Q K O P A H Z O Y C A A L E I P
F B N B T D L V I S R A E L I T E S Y T
K L E D H H T A P R O M I S E D L A N D
Y E S X I I W I N D W K B R O N Z E P Y
A U S C H A U N H C J A M R D P K T B H
```

Slithering Snakes

Use the snake code to solve the secret message

___ ___ ___ ___ and ___ ___ ___ ___ ___

Journal Page

Think about a time you felt dissatisfied or disappointed. Draw a picture or write a few sentences describing the situation. How could you be thankful for that same situation?

FAMILY DISCUSSION STARTERS
- How were the Israelites healed? (*They looked at the bronze snake.*)
- Can people save themselves from sin? (*No, only Jesus saves; John 14:6*)
- When someone in your family grumbles, stop and thank God for caring for you.

Across the Jordan

Number the stones from 1 to 12 to put the events from today's Bible story in the order that they happened. (We've done the first one for you.)
Tip: Need help? Read Joshua 2–4; 6 in your Bible.

- The Israelites shouted.
- Rahab tied a bright red rope in her window.
- The Israelites marched around Jericho.
- Joshua sent two spies into Jericho.
- The priests carried the ark of the covenant to the edge of the water.
- Joshua set up 12 stones as a reminder.
- All the people crossed the Jordan on dry ground.
- Rahab hid the spies on her roof.
- God told Joshua to go into Canaan. (1)
- The wall of Jericho fell down.
- The Israelites captured Jericho.
- The water stopped flowing.

Design a Boat

Imagine you and your family needs to cross a wide, deep river. What would you use? In the space below, design a boat to carry you across.

THE PROMISED LAND AND JERICHO 8

Journal Page

List several things that God has done to help you or your family. You may also list events from the Bible in which God helped His people. Remember, God takes care of His people!

FAMILY DISCUSSION STARTERS

- How many times did the Israelites march around Jericho? (See Joshua 6:3–4.)
- Who knocked down the wall of Jericho? (*God did.*)
- As a family, how can you give God glory for providing?

Something Is Missing

Fill in the missing consonants to complete today's main point.

_O_ _ _ _ _ _E_ _ _OD

_ _U_ IS_E_ _OU_ _ _

_ _A_ _A FO_ _O_ _I_

_I_ _I_. E_O_ E

A_ _ A_.

Hidden Treasures

Look at all the treasures hidden in the tent!
Can you find the silver coins, the bar of gold, and the robe?

Look For

Journal Page

Write about a time you wanted to or tried to hide from God. How did you feel? Why do you think people might want to hide from God? Is this a good idea? What can we do when we sin?

FAMILY DISCUSSION STARTERS
- What did Achan do wrong?
- What is the penalty for sin? (See Romans 6:23.)
- What should you do when you sin?

Legacy List

The word *legacy* means "something left to another person or group of people." How many words can you create using these letters?

LEGACY

Remember This!

Decode the message on the stone to find out what the Israelites promised they would do.

KEY

✖	A	◓	H	▲	L	◐	O
★	E	⊙	I	●	O	▢	
◖	P	▼	S	⌄	W	☁	Y

JOSHUA'S FINAL ENCOURAGEMENT

Journal Page

Imagine you could make a speech on national television. What would you say? List some points below. What do you think is the most important thing for people to know or remember?

_____
_____
_____
_____
_____
_____
_____
_____
_____
_____
_____
_____
_____
_____
_____

FAMILY DISCUSSION STARTERS
- What did Joshua remind the Israelites? (*He reminded them of all the things God had done for them.*)
- What legacy did Jesus leave for His followers? (See Matthew 28:18-20.)
- What has God done for your family? How will you remember to worship Him?

Semester 2 • The Gospel Project: Home Edition Grades 3-5 Workbook

13

Who's There?

Color in the even-numbered spaces. Then turn the page sideways to discover the name of one of Israel's first judges.

3	2	32	20	11
40	37	65	61	42
62	17	63	59	4
6	48	52	22	24
39	19	21	29	43
8	72	50	76	74
5	27	41	35	54
86	26	88	90	56
47	7	57	33	13
80	46	10	18	82
25	23	28	9	15
44	30	68	78	84
69	53	55	67	45
70	51	14	31	58
12	49	38	1	60
66	34	36	64	16

First Judges Quiz

Read Judges 2:6-10; 3:7-31. Circle the correct answers.

1. The Israelites needed a new leader because (Moses / Joshua) had died.

2. God raised up (Othniel / Samson) to rule as the first judge.

3. Each time a judge died, the Israelites (remembered / forgot about) God.

4. The king of Moab was a very (fat / thin) man.

5. Ehud killed the king of Moab with a (hammer / sword).

6. After Ehud escaped, he became the Israelites' (leader / servant).

7. The Israelites experienced (war / peace) for 80 years.

8. After Ehud died, God sent a third judge named (Peter / Shamgar).

THE FIRST JUDGES

14

Journal Page

The Israelites forgot about God, and God allowed their enemies to defeat them. List a few things you want to remember about God.

_____
_____
_____
_____
_____
_____
_____
_____
_____
_____
_____
_____
_____
_____

FAMILY DISCUSSION STARTERS
- What happened when a judge died? *(The Israelites forgot about God.)*
- Why did the Israelites disobey God? (See Judges 2:10.)
- How can your family remember what God has done?

Cross It Out

Cross out every third word. Then unscramble the remaining words to find the answer to the big picture question.

How does God accomplish His plan?

and	glory	Lord	our
people	plan	uses	for
battle	good	His	not

God ____ ____ ____ ____

Who Am I?

Match each description to the person from the Bible.

- Jael • — I was the commander of the Canaanite army.
- Deborah • — I killed an enemy of the Israelites.
- Sisera • — God called me to go to battle.
- Barak • — I ruled as judge over Israel.

DEBORAH AND BARAK

16

Journal Page

Write a short prayer or poem, confessing your sin to God and asking for His forgiveness.

FAMILY DISCUSSION STARTERS
- Who was responsible for the victory? (See Judges 4:6-7.)
- What does it mean to give glory to God? (*to acknowledge His greatness and to honor Him*)
- What do we need to be rescued from? Whom did God send to rescue us?

A Name for Gideon

Solve the code to discover how the Angel of the Lord called to Gideon.
Each number matches up with a letter of the alphabet. (1 = A, 2 = B, 3 = C, and so on)

"The Lord is with you, ___ ___ ___ ___ ___ ___ ___ ___ ___ ___ ___ ___."
                         13 9 7 8 20 25 23 1 18 18 9 15 18

Main Point Word Maze

Use the words of today's main point to fill in the crossword puzzle.

GIDEON 18

Journal Page

Write down something you like to do—even if you are not the best at it. Then write a few sentences about how you might do that task for the glory of God.

FAMILY DISCUSSION STARTERS

- How many men went to battle with Gideon? (See Judges 7:7.)
- Who was really responsible for the Israelites' victory?
- Read Ephesians 2:8-9. Who saves us from our sin?

Samson in Action

Look up each passage in your Bible. Write a short caption and illustrate the scene to complete the comic strip.

Judges 14:5

Judges 16:17-19

Judges 16:29-30

Who Am I? Riddles

Can you solve these riddles about people in the Bible? Look up the verses to check your answer!

THIS MAN MET WITH EGLON,
KING OF MOAB.
HE PULLED OUT HIS SWORD
AND GAVE HIM A JAB.
GOING ONTO THE PORCH
AND LOCKING THE DOOR,
HE LEFT THE KING THERE,
DEAD ON THE FLOOR!

WHO AM I? (SEE JUDGES 3:15-25.)

THERE ONCE WAS A WOMAN
WHO LIVED IN A TENT.
GOD USED HER FOR GLORY
IN ONE BIG EVENT.
WHEN THE ARMY COMMANDER
CAME IN FOR A SNOOZE,
SHE GAINED ISRAEL'S VICTORY
AND CANAAN DID LOSE.

WHO AM I? (SEE JUDGES 4:17-24.)

AN ANGEL APPEARED
UNDER A TREE
AND TOLD THIS MAN,
"A MIGHTY WARRIOR YOU'LL BE!"
THIS MAN TESTED GOD,
PUTTING FLEECE ON THE GROUND.
GOD CLEARLY WAS WITH HIM;
HE WAS ALWAYS AROUND!

WHO AM I? (SEE JUDGES 6:11-12.)

SAMSON

Journal Page

List three things you are good at. Thank God for your talent. Then write a few sentences about how you might use your skills to glorify God. (We glorify God when we show others how great He is.)

FAMILY DISCUSSION STARTERS

- Samson was supposed to rescue the Israelites from what people? (*the Philistines*)
- What was Samson not supposed to do? (See Judges 13:5.)
- Talk about a time you disobeyed. What were the consequences?

On the Move

Use markers or colored pencils to complete the instructions.

1. Color the seas blue.
2. Color the land yellow.
3. Circle the city of Bethlehem.
4. Draw a path from Bethlehem to the land of Moab.
5. Circle the land of Israel.
6. Draw a triangle at the city of Jericho.
7. Draw a star at the city of Jerusalem.

Gathering Grain

Collect the fallen grain. Leave behind any pieces that have a match. Circle the remaining pieces and then rearrange them to discover the main point.

Naomi, famine, home, famine, God, Naomi, field, Ruth, redeemer

grain, provided, home, Boaz, for, grain, Boaz, a, field

RUTH AND BOAZ 22

Journal Page

List people who provide for you or protect you. Be sure to thank those people for their care! Whom did God send to care for us in the greatest way?

FAMILY DISCUSSION STARTERS

- Who promised to take care of Ruth and her family? (*Boaz*)
- When Jesus redeems us, whose family are we adopted into? (*God's family, Galatians 4:5*)
- How can you show God's love to someone in need?

Semester 2 • The Gospel Project: Home Edition Grades 3-5 Workbook

Who Said That?

Match each saying to the person who said it. Look up the Scripture references in your Bible to check your answers!

"Speak, for Your servant is listening." (1 Samuel 3:10)

"We must go up and take possession of the land because we can certainly conquer it." (Numbers 13:30)

"Am I my brother's guardian?" (Genesis 4:9)

"You planned evil against me; God planned it for good." (Genesis 50:20)

"Who is Yahweh that I should obey Him?" (Exodus 5:2)

How Does He Do It?

Copy the words from the puzzle pieces into their correct places. Complete the puzzle to answer the big picture question: *How does God accomplish His plan?*

ELI AND BOY SAMUEL

Journal Page

Write a few sentences as a prayer to God, asking Him for something you desire.

FAMILY DISCUSSION STARTERS
- Does God always give us everything we desire? Why or why not?
- What did Hannah promise God? (See 1 Samuel 1:9-11.)
- Are you willing to listen for God and tell others about Him?

Donkey Roundup

Find and circle the 10 donkeys hidden in the picture. Round up 4 brown donkeys, 3 gray donkeys, 2 red donkeys, and 1 white donkey.

God Chose a King

Find the words hidden in the picture. Then arrange them to form the main point of the Bible story.

___ ___ ___ ___ ___ ___ ___ .

ISRAEL DEMANDED A KING

Journal Page

Write about a time you felt cared for or safe. Write a few sentences of prayer to God to thank Him for caring for you directly or for putting people in your life to take care of you.

FAMILY DISCUSSION STARTERS
- How was demanding a king the same as rejecting God?
- Do you think Saul wanted to be king? Why or why not?
- What does it mean for Jesus to be our King forever?

Rejected!

Cross out every third letter to find out what today's Bible story is about.

G O A D R I E J L E C
S T E M D S O A U K L
A N S K Y I N E G

Main Point Mix-Up

Unscramble the words of today's main point.

God of his as rejected Saul sin king because

___ ___ ___ ___ ___ ___ ___

Journal Page

Write about or draw a picture of a time you disobeyed God or someone God put in charge over you, such as a parent or teacher. What were the consequences of your actions?

FAMILY DISCUSSION STARTERS
- What do you think Saul really cared about with his sacrifice?
- Why is it hard to trust God when we have to wait for things that we want right away?
- Can you think of a King whom God will never reject?

Semester 2 • The Gospel Project: Home Edition Grades 3-5 Workbook

29

Facing a Giant

Use the scale to draw a picture of yourself next to Goliath. Goliath was more than 9 feet tall!

- height
- weight
- speed

The Goliath Quiz

Connect each question with the correct answer. If you need help, look up the Scripture in your Bible.

1. Whom did Samuel anoint to be king? (1 Samuel 16:13)
2. What people fought against Israel? (1 Samuel 17:1)
3. What did David use to kill Goliath? (1 Samuel 17:49)
4. Who gave David power to defeat Goliath? (1 Samuel 17:45-46)
5. Who is our King? (John 18:37)

a rock
David
God
the Philistines
Jesus

Journal Page

Draw a picture of or write about what you would do if you were king over a country. How do you feel knowing that Jesus is our King forever? How can you show you trust Him?

FAMILY DISCUSSION STARTERS
- Why do you think God chose David—a smaller, younger man?
- How did David know he could beat Goliath?
- Can you think of someone else who defeated a giant enemy on behalf of His people?

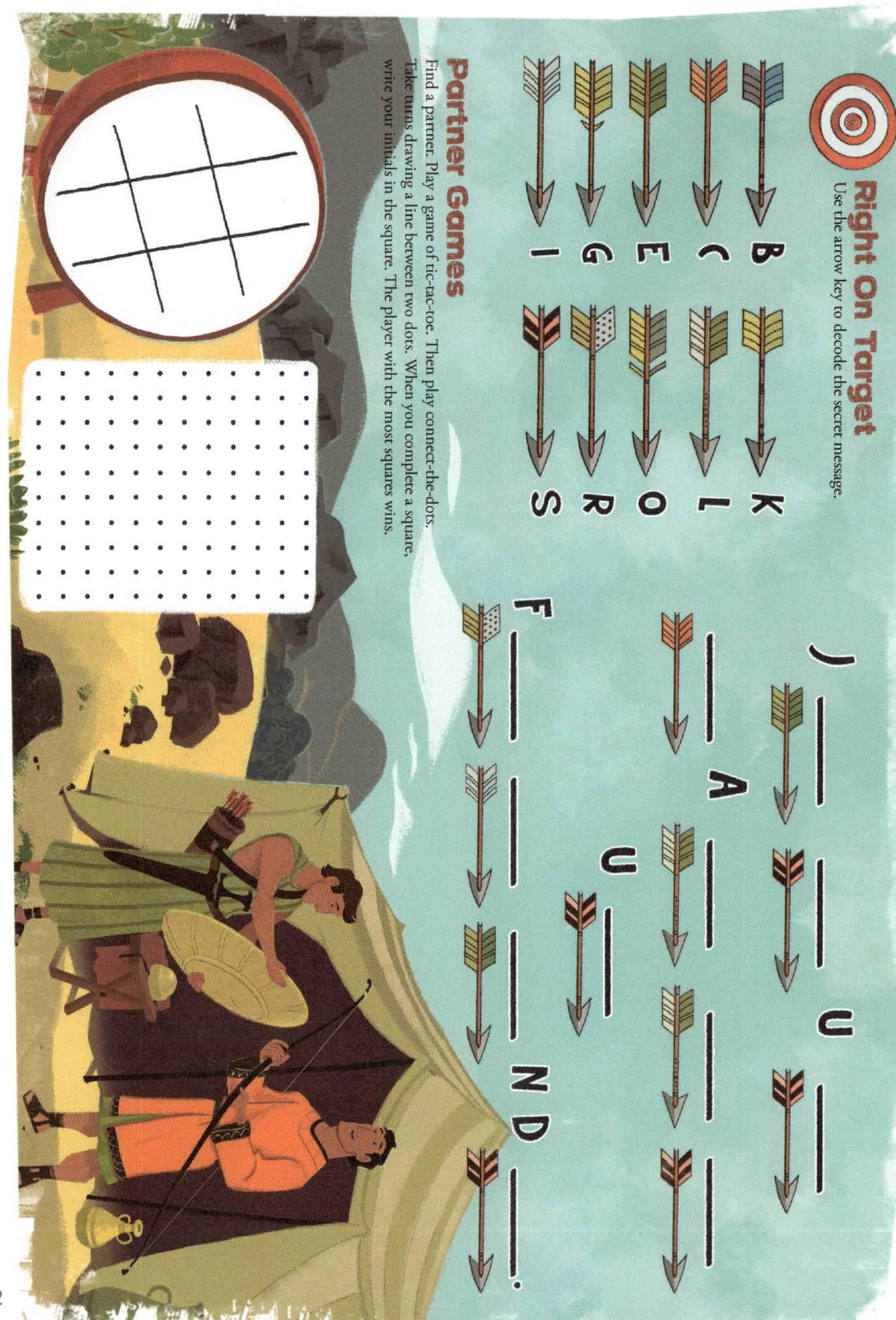

Journal Page

List a few friends you can pray for this week. How can you show them you love them and that God loves them too?

FAMILY DISCUSSION STARTERS
- What might have been hard for Jonathan to accept about David?
- What are some things Jonathan had to give up to help David?
- Who else gave up His place next to a throne to help us?

Word Choices

Choose the correct words to complete the story. If you need help, read 2 Samuel 7:11-13.

"The Lord Himself will make _____ (a house / breakfast) for you. When your time comes and you _____ (play / rest) with your fathers, I will raise up after you your _____ (pet / descendant), ... and I will establish his _____ (kingdom / schedule). He will build a _____ (tower / house) for My name, and I will establish the _____ (chair / throne) of his kingdom _____ (forever / for 50 years)."

Timeline Maze

Make your way through the maze. Which Bible people do you encounter?

Start — Adam — Abraham — Jacob — David — Jesus — Finish

GOD MADE A COVENANT WITH DAVID

34

Journal Page

Write about other people in your family who trust in Jesus. What have you learned from them? You may also list family members you would like to pray for.

FAMILY DISCUSSION STARTERS
- Why did David want to build a temple for God?
- Why do you think God stopped David from building a temple?
- How do you think David felt, knowing about God's promise to send the Messiah through David's family?

Alpha-baa-t Words

How many words can you create using the letters on the sheep?
What is the longest word you can create?

Letters on sheep: T, N, E, P, E, R

Life Events

Number the events in the order they happened in David's life.

KING DAVID

God made a covenant with David.

David and Jonathan became friends.

David was anointed and fought Goliath.

David sinned and was restored.

DAVID SINNED AND WAS RESTORED

36

Journal Page

Write a prayer to God, like David did in Psalm 51. Repent of your sin and ask for forgiveness through Jesus. You may also copy some of David's words in Psalm 51.

FAMILY DISCUSSION STARTERS
- Why is sin still bad even if you don't get caught?
- What ways can sin harm us or our relationships?
- How can we be sure God will forgive us of our sins?

What Would You Do?

Determine what is happening in each picture. What should you do in each scenario? How do you know what the right choice is?

A Better Way

Work from left to right. Color in the correct word in each column to complete the Bible story's main point.

Solomon	helped	angels	for	wisdom	and	race	his	house.
David	tried	God	from	knowledge	through	lead	their	people.
Samuel	asked	friends	about	questions	or	swim	God's	sheep.
Moses	called	enemies	by	ideas	to	follow	our	kingdom.

SOLOMON ASKED FOR WISDOM

38

Journal Page

Write about what you would like to ask God for and why. Then pray and ask Him! God hears our prayers. (See 1 John 5:14.)

FAMILY DISCUSSION STARTERS
- What do you think would have happened if Solomon had not asked for wisdom?
- Why do you think Solomon did not ask for the other things God gave him?
- What do you think would happen if we asked for wisdom, too?

Correct the Proverbs

These proverbs are not right! Find each reference in your Bible and rewrite the proverb to match God's Word.

The fear of the Lord is the beginning of foolishness; fools love wisdom and discipline.
Proverbs 1:7 _____

Trust in the Lord with all your mind, and sometimes rely on your own understanding.
Proverbs 3:5 _____

Guard your mind above all else, for it is the source of wisdom.
Proverbs 4:23 _____

Commit your thoughts to the Lord, and your plans will be achieved.
Proverbs 16:3 _____

The one who conceals his face will not prosper, but whoever confesses and renounces them will find mercy.
Proverbs 28:13 _____

Leave It to the Experts

Who would know best? Match each question to the expert who would likely know the best answer.

attorney   chef   pediatrician
master gardener   electrician   banker

$ How much money should I save?

🍎 Can I substitute apple sauce for oil in a recipe?

💡 How do I repair a light switch?

🌸 How often should I water my daffodils?

⚖️ Is it against the law to borrow something without asking?

🧒 What should I do when I have a stomachache?

BONUS: Who knows how life works best? _____

WISDOM FOR GOD'S PEOPLE

40

Journal Page

Write some words of wisdom you learned from the Bible. If you need help, review the Bible story or browse the Book of Proverbs for a wise saying. Who gives us wisdom when we ask?

FAMILY DISCUSSION STARTERS
- What is the difference between knowledge and wisdom?
- What do you think it means to fear the Lord?
- Can you usually trust what a wise person says?

Temple Quiz

Put a check mark next to each correct answer. Look up the Scripture references to see if you are right!

1. How many years after the Israelites left Egypt did Solomon build the temple? (1 Kings 6:1)
   - [ ] A. 48 years
   - [ ] B. 480 years
   - [ ] C. 4,800 years

2. How tall was the temple? (1 Kings 6:2)
   - [ ] A. 15 feet
   - [ ] B. 45 feet
   - [ ] C. 450 feet

3. Where was the temple located? (1 Kings 8:1)
   - [ ] A. Jerusalem
   - [ ] B. Jericho
   - [ ] C. Bethlehem

4. What filled the temple? (1 Kings 8:11)
   - [ ] A. water
   - [ ] B. fire
   - [ ] C. the glory of the Lord

5. How did the people feel about having a temple? (1 Kings 8:66)
   - [ ] A. joyful
   - [ ] B. afraid
   - [ ] C. confused

Solomon Built It | Connect the dots to discover what Solomon built.

SOLOMON BUILT THE TEMPLE

42

Journal Page

Write a few sentences describing how you feel knowing that you are never alone. Remember, God dwells with His people!

FAMILY DISCUSSION STARTERS
- What's the difference between a temple and our church buildings?
- Where does God live now?
- Why can we now approach God directly, without a priest or a temple?

Make It Whole

Can you complete the pictures? Draw the missing half of each object.

The Tribes of Israel

After the Israelites took over the promised land, the land was divided among the 12 tribes—the families of the sons of Jacob.

Rehoboam was the king of the Southern Kingdom (Judah).

Color these tribes yellow:
- Judah
- Benjamin
- Simeon

Jeroboam became the king of the Northern Kingdom (Israel).

Color these tribes red:
- West & East Manasseh
- Naphtali
- Ephraim
- Issachar
- Zebulun
- Reuben
- Asher
- Gad
- Dan

SOLOMON'S SIN DIVIDED THE KINGDOM

44

Journal Page

Write about a time you sinned. Were any of your relationships affected? Write a short prayer, thanking God for forgiving your sin and ask Him to restore any relationships affected by that sin.

FAMILY DISCUSSION STARTERS

- What happens if we trust God just half the time?
- What changed about God's love for Solomon when he stopped obeying God?
- David and Solomon both made big mistakes; can you think of a King who never sinned?

The Story of Job

Find and circle the following words.

children
control
curse
doubt
eagles
earth
Elihu
faith
good
Job
powerful
Satan
sea
sin
sky
sovereign
stars
suffering
trust
wealth
whirlwind

```
U S E A L Y S H E G
Z A G T U K U T D O
B T F S F R A O O
B A W U R G F A E D
O N H R E W E E L E
J H I T W L R E I C
L T R K O I A H H
X L L H P R N G U I
O A W T S T G L B L
G E I N N M E C D
S W N A J O W S K R
R H D F Y C T C K E
A S O V E R E I G N
T C U R S E F T X R
S C D O U B T U Q I
```

God is ___

Unscramble the key words from the Bible story main point. Then match each word with its definition.

LLA-ROWELPUF

having the highest power or authority. God is above all things and in control of all things.

RINGEESOV

right, kind, loyal; the opposite of bad. God always does what is right, for His glory.

DOGO

having complete, unlimited power or authority. God can do all things.

JOB
46

Journal Page

Write a letter to yourself that you can read when you are suffering. Write things you know to be true about God.

FAMILY DISCUSSION STARTERS
- Who is always in control, even in hard times?
- How can we know that God is good?
- How do you think Job felt after God spoke with him?

On Purpose

Match the items that go together to figure out why the objects on the left exist.

Solomon Crossword

Solve the crossword puzzle. Then unscramble the circled letters to complete a very important message!

ACROSS
4. What book comes before Ecclesiastes?
5. What did God give Solomon?

DOWN
1. What book of the Bible records Solomon's thoughts about life?
2. Who was the king of Israel after David?
3. Who is God the Son?
4. What book comes before Proverbs?

WORDS: Ecclesiastes Jesus Proverbs Psalms Solomon wisdom

Jesus gives us P _ _ _ _ _ _ for living.

SOLOMON THOUGHT ABOUT LIFE
48

Journal Page

List any questions you have about life, people, or God. Who knows how life works best? Who has a plan for your life? Do you trust Him?

FAMILY DISCUSSION STARTERS
- What are some things about life that you struggle to understand?
- How does it make you feel to know God is in control, even when life is confusing?
- What does God say is the purpose of our lives?

Journal Page

Read Psalm 100 in the Bible. Write a few lines of your own to express your love for the Lord and your trust in Him.

FAMILY DISCUSSION STARTERS
- What kind of music do you like most? Happy songs? Fast songs? Loud songs?
- Have you ever sung a song to God to help you express yourself to Him?
- Why do you think God likes to hear our praises?

Joshua and Caleb
Numbers 13:1–14:38

MAIN POINT: THE ISRAELITES DID NOT TRUST GOD TO GIVE THEM THE PROMISED LAND.

God told Moses, "Send men to scout out the land of Canaan (KAY nuhn). I am giving this land to the Israelites."

So the men went and scouted out the land. They traveled around the land for 40 days. Then they went back to Moses, Aaron, and the Israelite community to tell them what they saw.

"The land is good," they said. "But the people living in the land are strong, and the cities they live in are large and well protected."

Then Caleb, one of the spies, said, "We must go up and take possession of the land! We can certainly conquer it with God's help!"

But the other men disagreed. "We can't go up against the people! They are stronger than we are. We looked like grasshoppers compared to them!"

The Israelites were afraid, and they cried all night. The Israelites said, "Let's appoint a new leader and go back to Egypt!"

Joshua and Caleb, who had both scouted out the land, said to the Israelites, "Don't be afraid of the people living in the land; God is with us!"

God threatened to destroy all the people, but Moses said, "Please forgive the wrongdoing of the people. I know You are great, faithful, and loving."

God replied, "Since you have asked, I will forgive them. But they will not live to see the promised land of Canaan." Since Caleb and Joshua followed God completely, God let them enter the promised land. God said that the Israelites would wander in the wilderness 40 years. They would not enter the promised land.

Christ Connection: Caleb and Joshua trusted God. God planned for Joshua to lead the next generation of Israelites into the promised land. Joshua was not perfect, but His faithfulness reminds us of Jesus, who is perfect. Jesus obeyed the Father and trusted His plan to save people from their sins.

The Bronze Snake
Numbers 20:1-20; 21:4-9

MAIN POINT: GOD TOLD HIS PEOPLE TO LOOK AT THE BRONZE SNAKE TO BE HEALED.

The Israelites refused to go into the promised land, so God punished them and made them wander in the wilderness. When the Israelites set up camp, they complained that they did not have water to drink. God told Moses and Aaron to stand in front of all the people and speak to a rock. God said water would come out of the rock.

Instead of talking to the rock, Moses hit the rock two times with his staff. The water came out, but God was angry that Moses and Aaron disobeyed Him. God said Moses and Aaron would not lead the Israelites into the promised land.

The Israelites continued through the wilderness. The journey was long, and they grumbled and complained.

God sent poisonous snakes that bit the Israelites, and many of the people died. They realized they had sinned by complaining to God.

Moses spoke to God for them. Then God told Moses, "Make a snake image and put it on a pole. When anyone who is bitten looks at it, he will recover."

Moses made a bronze snake and mounted it on a pole. Whenever someone was bitten, that person looked at the bronze snake, and he recovered.

Christ Connection: The Israelites faced a huge problem because of their sin. God sent snakes to punish Israel, but anyone who was bitten could look at the snake on the pole and live. Because of our sin, we face a huge problem: we are separated from God. We deserve to die, but anyone who looks to Jesus on the cross and trusts in Him will live forever with God.

The Promised Land and Jericho
Joshua 2–4; 6

MAIN POINT: GOD FOUGHT FOR HIS PEOPLE AND LED THEM INTO THE PROMISED LAND.

When Moses died, Joshua became the leader of the Israelites. God told Joshua it was time to go into the land God promised to give Abraham's family. Other people lived in the land, so the Israelites had to defeat them.

Joshua sent two spies into Jericho to check it out. They stayed at the house of a woman named Rahab. Rahab hid the men on her roof to keep them safe.

The spies promised to keep Rahab and her family safe when the Israelites came into the city. Then the spies left Jericho.

Now the Israelites traveled toward the Jordan River, which separated them from the promised land. The people got ready to cross. The priests carried the ark of the covenant to the edge of the water. Then the priests stepped into the water, and the river stopped. All the people crossed the Jordan on dry ground.

Joshua set up a reminder that God stopped the water and helped them cross the river.

Next, God told Joshua, "March around the city one time each day for six days. On the seventh day, march around the city seven times. Then all the people should shout, and the walls of Jericho will fall down. The Israelites can then go into the city and conquer it."

Joshua did what God said. On the seventh day, they marched around the city seven times. The people shouted, and the wall fell down. The Israelites went into the city and captured it. They destroyed everything in the city, but Rahab and her family were safe.

Christ Connection: God fought for His people and led them into the promised land. Just as the Lord defeated Jericho for the Israelites, Jesus defeats His enemies and leads believers into the promised land of eternity.

Achan's Sin and the Defeat of Ai
Joshua 7–8

MAIN POINT: GOD PUNISHED ACHAN FOR HIS SIN. THEN GOD FOUGHT FOR HIS PEOPLE AT AI.

The Lord had helped the Israelites take over the city of Jericho. He had given them specific instructions about what to do with everything in the city. But the Israelites did not obey God completely. They kept some things for themselves, and God knew. So when the Israelites attacked the city of Ai, God did not fight for them and Israel lost the battle.

God said to Joshua, "Israel has sinned. They took some of the things I told them not to. This is why they cannot defeat their enemies."

The next day, the Israelites came together and God showed Joshua which man had sinned. The man's name was Achan. Achan confessed that he had taken from Jericho a beautiful cloak, some pieces of silver, and a bar of gold.

After Achan was punished for his sin, God told Joshua to attack Ai again. This time, God promised to give them victory over the city.

The king of Ai sent out his men to fight. When the enemy army got near, Joshua and the Israelites pretended to be afraid, so the army of Ai chased them away from the city.

Joshua held out his sword, and the Israelite men who were hiding behind the city took over the city. This time, the Israelites did just what God said.

Christ Connection: The punishment for Achan's sin was death. It seems harsh, but the Bible says that the wages of sin is death. (Romans 6:23) Because we sin, we deserve to die too. Jesus came to die in our place. When we confess our sins and trust in Jesus, we are forgiven and saved from spiritual death.

Joshua's Final Encouragement
Joshua 23:1–24:28

MAIN POINT: JOSHUA ENCOURAGED THE PEOPLE TO WORSHIP GOD ALONE.

Joshua was getting old and knew he would die soon. He gathered all the people of Israel because he had some important things to say to them.

Joshua said, "Be careful to obey everything that is in the book of the law of Moses. You will die here if you disobey Him."

Joshua reminded all the people about the things God had done for them in the past. Joshua told the people about how God had rescued the Israelites from the Egyptians. God had done so many great things for His people!

"Fear the Lord and worship Him," he said.

The people replied, "We know how much God has done for us, and we love Him!" The people said, "We will worship Yahweh!"

On that day, Joshua made a covenant with the people. He set up a large stone under an oak tree.

Joshua said, "This stone will be a reminder of your duty to serve the Lord, who fulfilled every promise in bringing you into this land."

Christ Connection: As Joshua prepared for his own death, he left a legacy of obedience to God. After Jesus' death and resurrection, He appeared to the disciples and left them with a legacy: to make disciples of all nations, baptizing them in the name of the Father and of the Son and of the Holy Spirit, teaching them to obey everything Jesus commanded. (Matthew 28:19-20)

The First Judges
Judges 3:7-31

MAIN POINT: GOD'S PEOPLE TURNED FROM HIM TO WORSHIP IDOLS.

Joshua had died. Without a strong leader, the Israelites began to disobey God and worship false gods. God let an enemy king take over the Israelites.

Then the Israelites remembered how good they had it when they loved and obeyed God. They cried out to Him, "Save us!" God raised up Othniel to rule over them as the first judge. The land was peaceful for 40 years, then Othniel died.

Again, Israel forgot about God. God gave the king of Moab power to attack the Israelites and defeat them. The Israelites remembered how good they had it when they loved and obeyed God. They cried out to Him, "Save us!" So God raised up Ehud to save them.

The Israelites sent Ehud to the king of Moab. Ehud said, "I have a secret message for you." The king dismissed all his attendants so he was alone with Ehud.

When the king stood up, Ehud pulled out his sword. He pushed it into the king's belly. Ehud escaped down the porch, locking the doors of the room behind him. The king's servants came in and found their king dead!

When Ehud escaped, he blew a ram's horn and he became the Israelites' leader. There was peace in the land for 80 years.

When Ehud died, the Israelites forgot God again. They turned away from Him. When they remembered how good they had it when the loved and obeyed God, they cried out to Him, "Save us!" God sent a third judge, Shamgar, to save them.

Christ Connection: The judges saved the people from the consequences of their sin, but not the cause of it. God's plan was to one day send a true Deliverer—Jesus, His own Son—to be the King of His people. Jesus saves people from sin forever.

54

Deborah and Barak
Judges 4–5

MAIN POINT: GOD'S PEOPLE NEEDED SOMEONE TO RESCUE THEM FROM THEIR ENEMIES.

Ehud and Shamgar had been judges over Israel. After they died, the Israelites forgot about God. So God allowed the king of Canaan to overtake them. The commander of the king's army was named Sisera. Sisera was cruel to the Israelites for 20 years. God's people remembered how good they had it when they loved and obeyed God. They cried out to God, "Save us!"

Deborah was the judge over Israel. One day, Deborah called for Barak and said, "God wants you to gather 10,000 men. God will help you defeat Sisera." Barak said to Deborah, "I will go if you will come with me. If you won't come, I'm not going."

"I'll go," Deborah said. "But you will receive no honor for the battle."

Barak and his 10,000 men moved down the mountain toward Sisera and his army. The Lord confused Sisera and all of the army. Barak chased the chariots and the army. None of them survived, but Sisera escaped!

Sisera went to the tent of Jael. Jael gave Sisera something to drink and covered him with a rug. Sisera was so exhausted that he fell into a deep sleep. Jael knew that Sisera was an evil man, an enemy of God. She killed him while he slept.

That day, God allowed the Israelites to defeat the Canaanites. The Israelites had won the battle! Deborah and Barak praised God for helping them beat the Canaanites. The land was peaceful for 40 more years.

Christ Connection: God does what is for His glory and our good. (Psalm 115:3; Romans 8:28) God fought for the Israelites and used Deborah, Barak, and Jael to defeat Canaan. In a similar way, God uses people and events to not only save us from our enemies, but to bring about our ultimate good: salvation through His Son, Jesus Christ.

Gideon
Judges 6–8

MAIN POINT: GOD USED GIDEON'S WEAKNESS FOR HIS GLORY.

The Israelites did what is evil in the sight of the Lord, so God allowed them to be ruled by their enemies, the Midianites. The Midianites were very mean to them, so the Israelites cried out to God, "Save us!"

The Angel of the Lord appeared to a man named Gideon and said, "The Lord is with you, mighty warrior!" The Lord chose Gideon to deliver the Israelites from the power of their enemy. He assured Gideon, "I will be with you."

Some time later, Israel's enemies gathered together. An army of men gathered behind Gideon, ready to fight. Gideon still wanted a sign from God. "If You will deliver Israel by my hand, as You say, I will put fleece on the ground. If the fleece is wet with dew, but the ground is dry, I will believe You."

That is exactly what happened! Again, Gideon asked for a sign. This time, the fleece was dry and the ground was wet.

God told Gideon that he had too many people with him. God made a test for the people. All of them were to go to the river to drink the water. Anyone who knelt to drink water was sent home, but whoever lapped the water with his tongue stayed. Three hundred men remained.

The next day, the army carried torches, blew their trumpets, and shattered pitchers before running toward the camp of Midianites. God gave Israel the victory. But after Gideon died, the Israelites did not remember the Lord, who had delivered them from the power of their enemies.

Christ Connection: The Israelites cried out to God because they knew they could not save themselves. Even Gideon was not enough to save them; God used Gideon to save His people, but God fought the battle for them. The people needed someone who was mighty to save. Jesus Christ came to save us from sin because we cannot save ourselves. Only God, through Christ, can save us.

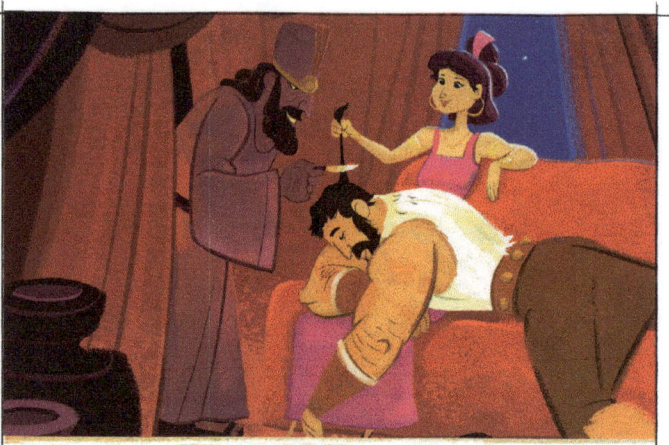

Samson
Judges 13–16

MAIN POINT: GOD GAVE SAMSON POWER.

The Israelites disobeyed God, so God let the Philistines rule over them. One day, the Angel of the Lord appeared to Manoah and his wife. He told them they would have a son who would save the Israelites from the Philistines. God had special instructions for their son, Samson: He should never cut his hair.

God blessed Samson and made him strong. When Samson grew up, he saw a Philistine woman he wanted to marry. On the journey to meet her, a lion jumped out at Samson. Samson killed the lion. When Samson and his parents returned for the wedding, Samson found the lion. Bees had made honey in the lion's body.

Samson told the Philistine men a riddle: *Out of the eater came something to eat, and out of the strong came something sweet.* The riddle was about the lion and the honey, but the men could not figure it out. They asked Samson's new wife for help. Samson told his wife the answer, and she told the men. Samson had been tricked! He was angry and left. When he went back to get his wife, she was gone.

Later, Samson fell in love with a woman named Delilah. The Philistines offered Delilah money if she would find out why Samson was so strong.

Samson told Delilah, "If you cut my hair, I will not have my strength." So when Samson was sleeping, the Philistines cut his hair. Samson wasn't strong anymore. The Philistines grabbed him and took him away in chains.

One day, the Philistines made Samson stand between two pillars in their temple. Samson cried out to God, "Lord, please strengthen me once more." God strengthened Samson. Samson pushed on the pillars and collapsed the temple. Samson and everyone in the temple died.

Christ Connection: Samson's sin led to his own death, but God used his death to deliver the Israelites from their enemies. Samson's story reminds us of Jesus. Jesus never sinned, but God sent Him to die on the cross and rise again to rescue believers from sin and give them eternal life.

Ruth and Boaz
Ruth 1–4

MAIN POINT: GOD PROVIDED A REDEEMER FOR RUTH.

Naomi lived in Bethlehem in Judah with her husband and their two sons. There was a famine in the land, so Naomi and her husband decided to go to Moab. While they were in Moab, Naomi's husband died. Naomi's sons married women from Moab, Orpah and Ruth. They lived in Moab for 10 years, and then Naomi's sons died. The famine was over, so Naomi decided to go home.

Orpah returned home, but Ruth clung to Naomi. "Wherever you go, I will go, and wherever you live, I will live; your people will be my people, and your God will be my God," Ruth said. So Naomi and Ruth returned to Bethlehem.

Naomi gave Ruth permission to go into the fields and gather fallen grain. She happened to go to the field of Boaz, a good man from the family of Naomi's late husband. Boaz told Ruth to stay in his field where she would be safe. Boaz made sure Ruth had enough food.

Ruth told Naomi about Boaz. "Boaz is one of our family redeemers," Naomi replied. A *family redeemer* was someone who would help his close relatives if they were in trouble. Naomi knew Boaz would take care of Ruth, so she encouraged Ruth to stay in his fields.

Boaz promised to redeem Ruth, which meant he would buy back the land that Naomi sold after her husband died, and he would marry Ruth.

Boaz bought back the land that had belonged to Naomi's family, and he married Ruth. Ruth and Boaz had a son named Obed.

Christ Connection: Boaz was a family redeemer. That means he would help his close relatives who were in trouble. Boaz cared for Ruth and Naomi because their husbands had died. In a similar way, Jesus is our Redeemer. We need help because we sin. Jesus bought our salvation for us by taking our punishment when He died on the cross.

Eli and Boy Samuel
1 Samuel 1–3

MAIN POINT: GOD CALLED SAMUEL TO SHARE GOD'S PLAN.

A man named Elkanah lived with his wife Hannah. Hannah was very sad because she did not have any children. Every year, Elkanah went to the tabernacle to make sacrifices to worship God. Hannah went with him.

Hannah prayed to God, "Lord, if You give me a son, I will dedicate him to You. He will serve You all of his life." A priest named Eli sat near the doorpost of the tabernacle. Eli watched Hannah pray and thought something wrong.

Hannah explained, "I've been pouring out my heart before the Lord."

Eli replied, "Go in peace. May God answer your prayers."

God did answer her prayers and Hannah gave birth to a son. She named him Samuel. When Samuel was no longer a baby, Hannah took him to Eli at the tabernacle. Hannah returned home and left Samuel with Eli to serve God. Samuel grew older and found favor with God and with men.

One night, Eli was in his bed and Samuel was lying in the tabernacle when Samuel heard someone speak to him. Samuel ran to Eli. "Here I am; you called me." God called Samuel three times, Each time Samuel ran to Eli. "Here I am," he said. Eli finally understood that God was calling Samuel. He told Samuel how to respond. Samuel went back to his place, and God called, "Samuel, Samuel!"

"Speak, for Your servant is listening," Samuel replied. God told Samuel that He was going to judge Eli's family for their sin.

The next day, Samuel was afraid to tell Eli what God had said. Eli asked Samuel to tell him what God said, so Samuel did. As Samuel grew, God was with him. God used Samuel to share His plan with the nation of Israel.

Christ Connection: Samuel used God's words to tell the people what God is like. John 1:1 says that Jesus is the Word. Jesus showed the world what God is like, and He told people to turn away from their sin. Jesus ultimately freed people from the power of sin by dying on the cross and rising again.

Israel Demanded a King
1 Samuel 8–10

MAIN POINT: GOD CHOSE SAUL AS ISRAEL'S FIRST KING.

Samuel was a judge over Israel. He had two sons, Joel and Abijah. Joel and Abijah were not good judges like their father was.

The leaders of Israel went to Samuel. "We don't want them to lead us; we want a king like the nations around us!"

Samuel wasn't sure how to respond, so he prayed to God.

God said, "Samuel, they are not rejecting you; they are rejecting Me as king."

Samuel warned the people that they would regret asking for a king, but the Israelites didn't care. "Give us a king!" they said.

Meanwhile, a wealthy man named Kish was looking for some of his donkeys that had wandered off. Kish told his son Saul to take a servant with him and search for the missing animals. Saul searched, but he was unable to find the donkeys.

"Wait," his servant said. "There is a man of God in this city. Let's talk to him; maybe he knows where we can find the donkeys." Saul and his servant found the man of God—it was Samuel.

"Don't worry about the donkeys," Samuel said. "They have been found."

Samuel invited Saul to have dinner with him. The next morning, Samuel told Saul that God had chosen Saul to be the king of Israel.

Samuel used oil to anoint Saul. "You will be king!" Samuel said.

Some time later, Samuel gathered the Israelites to introduce Saul, their new king. Saul stood among all the people. "Long live the king!" they said.

Christ Connection: God intended for a heavenly king to rule over Israel, but the Israelites did not trust God's plan. So God chose Saul to be their king. God had a plan to one day send His Son, Jesus, to rule the entire world. Jesus would be the perfect King who would bring peace and salvation to the world.

God Rejected Saul as King
1 Samuel 13:1-14; 15:1-35

MAIN POINT: GOD REJECTED SAUL AS KING BECAUSE OF HIS SIN.

Saul gathered an army. The Philistines, enemies of Israel, were in the land. The Philistines came out to fight the Israelites. The Israelites were outnumbered. They were all afraid; some of them hid.

Saul wanted to ask God for help. Maybe if he made an offering to God, they would win the battle. But only the priests were allowed to give offerings to God. Saul waited for Samuel, but Samuel did not come. Saul decided to make an offering to God himself.

Then Samuel showed up. "Saul, what are you doing?" Samuel asked.

"I wanted to ask for God's help before we went into battle," Saul replied.

"You have disobeyed God," Samuel said. "You will not be king much longer. God is going to find someone obedient to be king."

Some time later, God wanted Saul to attack the Amalekites. God said to kill all of the people and all of the animals. So Saul and his army fought the Amalekites. They won, but they did not destroy everything like God commanded. Saul only destroyed the worthless things and things he didn't want.

Samuel confronted Saul. "I did obey Him!" Saul argued. "I only saved the best animals to sacrifice to the Lord."

"You rejected His instruction, so God has rejected you as king."

Saul admitted his sin and pleaded for forgiveness. God was sorry He had made Saul the king of Israel.

Christ Connection: King Saul sinned by giving a sacrifice that only the priest was allowed to give. God rejected Saul as king, but He had a plan to send His Son, Jesus. King Jesus gave up His own life as a good and perfect sacrifice so sinners would be forgiven and accepted.

David Was Anointed and Fought Goliath
1 Samuel 16–17

MAIN POINT: GOD GAVE DAVID POWER TO DEFEAT GOLIATH.

God was going to give Israel a new king. God told Samuel to visit a man in Bethlehem named Jesse. God said one of Jesse's sons would be Israel's next king. Jesse's oldest son was tall and handsome.

"Samuel, he's not the one," God said. "Do not pay attention to what he looks like. You look at what you can see on the outside, but I see the heart."

One by one, Jesse's sons approached Samuel, but God had not chosen them.

Jesse said, "My youngest son, David, is in the field taking care of the sheep." Jesse sent for David. When David arrived, God told Samuel, "He's the one!" Samuel poured oil on David's head to show God had chosen him to be the king.

At this time, the Philistines—enemies of Israel—got ready for war. King Saul got his army ready to fight. The Philistines had a great warrior named Goliath. Goliath shouted at the Israelites, "Send me your best man, and we'll fight one-on-one." But none of the Israelites wanted to fight Goliath.

David saw Goliath and watched the Israelites run away in fear. So David volunteered to fight.

David explained, "God will keep me safe." David chose five smooth stones from a nearby stream. David was armed with only the stones and a slingshot.

"You come to fight with a spear and sword," David replied, "but I come to fight in the name of God! God always wins His battles!"

David slung a rock and hit Goliath in the forehead. Goliath fell facedown, and David killed him.

Christ Connection: David was not a big or strong warrior, but he trusted God. God gave David power. When God sent His Son to earth, Jesus did not look like a strong warrior either. But by dying on the cross and coming back to life, Jesus showed His power to save sinners.

David and Jonathan Became Friends
1 Samuel 18:1-12; 19:1-10; 20:1-42

MAIN POINT: GOD USED JONATHAN TO SAVE DAVID'S LIFE.

David lived at the king's palace. King Saul's son Jonathan became best friends with David. Jonathan gave gifts to David: his robe, military tunic, sword, bow, and belt.

Saul was jealous of David's success, and he wanted to kill David.

Jonathan asked Saul, "Why would you want to kill David? He has done nothing but help you." Saul promised not to kill David.

But King Saul did not keep His promise long. One day when David was playing the harp for Saul, Saul threw a spear at David. David escaped and told Jonathan what had happened.

"How can I help?" Jonathan asked.

David came up with a plan. Jonathan went to the special meal with his father. When Saul sat down to eat, he asked, "Where's David?"

"David is in Bethlehem. I gave him permission to go," Jonathan said.

Saul became angry. "David deserves to die!" he yelled.

Jonathan went to the field where David was hiding. He shot three arrows and sent his servant to retrieve them.

"The arrow is beyond you!" Jonathan shouted. That was Jonathan's sign to David that Saul wanted to kill him. David came out of hiding. David and Jonathan cried and said their goodbyes.

"Take care of yourself," Jonathan said. The two men parted ways knowing that no matter what, they would always be friends.

Christ Connection: David and Jonathan were true friends. Their friendship points to an even greater friendship—our friendship with Jesus. Jesus calls us friends (John 15:15), and He showed His love by dying to save us from sin.

God Made a Covenant with David
2 Samuel 7

MAIN POINT: GOD PROMISED THAT JESUS WOULD COME FROM DAVID'S FAMILY.

God chose David to be king of Israel. One day, David was talking with Nathan the prophet. David wanted to build a temple for the ark of God. He told Nathan his plans.

"God is with you. Do what you want!" Nathan said. That night, God gave Nathan a message for David.

"David, are you going to build a house for Me to live in? Did I ever ask anyone to build a temple for Me? You used to be a shepherd, David. But I made you a king. I promise you, David, that you and your descendants will be kings. When you die, one of your sons will be king. He will build a house for Me. The king will always be someone in your family."

Nathan told David everything God said. David went into the tent he had set up for the ark of the Lord. He sat down and prayed.

"God, You are so great! There is no one like You! Please keep Your promises to me and my descendants. I am confident You will keep Your promises because You are trustworthy."

Christ Connection: God promised David that every future king of Israel would come from David's family, and David's kingdom would last forever. God kept His promise by sending His Son, Jesus, to be one of David's descendants. Jesus is our King who will rule over God's people forever.

Semester 2 • The Gospel Project: Home Edition Grades 3-5 Workbook

David Sinned and Was Restored
2 Samuel 11:1–12:14; Psalm 51

MAIN POINT: GOD FORGAVE DAVID WHEN HE REPENTED OF HIS SIN.

David was the king of Israel. One spring, David sent out the army. David stayed in Jerusalem.

One evening, David looked out from the roof of his palace and saw a beautiful woman named Bathsheba. Bathsheba was the wife of Uriah, one of the best warriors in David's army. Bathsheba came to David's house. Later, Bathsheba told David that she was going to have a baby; the baby would be David's. David knew what he had done was wrong.

David called Uriah home from the battle and told him to go spend time with his wife. But Uriah slept on David's doorstep and refused to see his wife.

David's plan was not working, so he instructed Joab, who was leading the army, to send Uriah into the hardest part of the battle so he would be killed. Uriah was killed.

God knew what David had done, and He was not happy with David. God sent Nathan the prophet to talk to David.

David realized he had sinned against God. David deserved to die.

David confessed his sin and prayed, "God, create a clean heart for me." God wanted David's heart to change so that he would not want to sin again.

Christ Connection: When David sinned against God, God forgave him, but sin always comes with a price. God spared David's life, but David's son died. When we sin, we can receive God's forgiveness because God sent His Son, Jesus, to pay the price for our sin. Jesus died the death we deserve so that we could be made right with God.

Solomon Asked for Wisdom
1 Kings 2:1-4,10-12; 3:1-15

MAIN POINT: SOLOMON ASKED GOD FOR WISDOM TO LEAD GOD'S PEOPLE.

David had been the king of Israel for many years, and now his son Solomon was going to be king. Before David died, he gave Solomon some instructions.

David said, "Obey God, and you will be successful. God will keep His promise that every king of Israel will come from our family." When David died, Solomon became the king of Israel.

One night, God appeared to Solomon in a dream. God said, "Solomon, ask for anything you want, and I will give it to you."

Solomon prayed, "God, please make me wise and obedient to You. Help me know the difference between right and wrong. Help me lead Your people well."

God was happy with Solomon's request. God said, "I will give you wisdom."

Then God said, "Because you asked for wisdom, I will also give you what you did not ask for: long life, riches, and honor."

Solomon woke up and realized God had spoken to him in a dream.

Christ Connection: Solomon was a wise king who wanted to do God's plan. God planned to give His people a greater and wiser king—His Son, Jesus. Jesus completely trusted God with His life. Jesus surrendered His own life to die on the cross for our sin.

Wisdom for God's People
Proverbs 1:1-7; 3:1-12; 4:10-19

MAIN POINT: WISDOM IS FEARING THE LORD AND OBEYING HIS WORD.

King Solomon asked God to make him wise, so God gave Solomon wisdom. Solomon wrote down many wise sayings in the Book of Proverbs to help people live wisely. These are some of the words Solomon wrote.

"These proverbs are good for teaching you wisdom, for giving you understanding, and for leading you to what is right, honest, and fair. If you really want to be wise, begin by fearing the Lord. Only foolish people ignore wisdom and instruction.

"Never let go of love and truth. Then you will find favor with God and with man.

"Trust in the Lord with all your heart, and do not rely on your own understanding; think about Him in all your ways and He will guide you on the right path.

"Honor God with everything you have, and give Him the first and the best.

"God trains those He loves, like a father trains his son.

"Listen to my advice. I am teaching you how to be wise. Stay away from people who do evil. They hurt others and make foolish decisions. But a wise person is like the sun in the morning. They shine brighter throughout the day. A foolish person is like darkness. They can't even see what makes them trip and fall."

Christ Connection: Wisdom comes from God. He made the world and knows how it works best. Everyone is born a foolish sinner, but God sent His Son to earth to save us. The Bible says that Jesus is the wisdom of God. Jesus makes us wise and holy. He frees us from sin. (1 Cor. 1:24,30)

Solomon Built the Temple
1 Kings 6–8

MAIN POINT: GOD CHOSE SOLOMON TO BUILD A TEMPLE WHERE HE WOULD DWELL WITH HIS PEOPLE.

Solomon began to build a temple for the Lord. Solomon ordered thousands of workers to help build the temple.

God blessed the temple and made a promise to Solomon: "If you obey My commands, I will keep the promise I made to David. I will live among the Israelites, and I will not abandon My people."

The construction of the temple took seven more years. The craftsmanship was remarkable!

Now that the temple was complete, it was time for Solomon to move the ark of God from its place on Mount Zion to the new temple in Jerusalem. As the priests moved the ark, its holy utensils, and the tent of meeting, King Solomon and everyone who had gathered sacrificed sheep and cattle to the Lord.

The priests put the ark of the covenant in the most holy place in the temple. When the priests came out of the temple, a cloud filled the temple. God's glory was in the cloud.

Solomon turned to speak to the Israelites. "God promised David that his son would build a temple. God kept His promise!"

Solomon stood and prayed with his hands spread out toward heaven. "There is no God like You!" he said.

When Solomon had finished praying, he turned toward the Israelites and encouraged them to love and obey God.

Christ Connection: Because God is holy, only the priests could approach God—and only if they followed specific instructions. Ordinary people had no direct access to the holy presence of God. Jesus changed all that. By His death on the cross, Jesus took away our sin. We can approach God intimately and individually when we trust Jesus as Lord and Savior.

Solomon's Sin Divided the Kingdom
1 Kings 11–12

MAIN POINT: GOD DIVIDED ISRAEL INTO TWO KINGDOMS BECAUSE SOLOMON SINNED.

King Solomon loved God, but he did not love God with his whole heart. Solomon's wives turned him away from God. Solomon began to worship the false gods that his wives worshiped.

This made God angry. God said to Solomon, "Since you have done this, I will take the kingdom away from you. You will be king the rest of your life, but when your son becomes king, he will lose everything except for one tribe."

When Solomon died, his son Rehoboam became king. The people told Rehoboam, "Your father, Solomon, made us work too hard. We will gladly serve you if you make our work easier."

Rehoboam replied, "My father, Solomon, did not make you work hard enough! I'll make you work even harder!" God's people did not want to serve a king like Rehoboam, so they made Jeroboam, Solomon's official, the king. Only one tribe remained under Rehoboam's rule, and that was the southern tribe of Judah.

Jeroboam was now the king of Israel. He made two golden calves and made an announcement to the people. "It is very inconvenient for you to travel all the way to Jerusalem to worship at the temple," he said. "Look! These golden calves are the gods who brought your ancestors out of Egypt. You can worship them."

What Jeroboam did was a sin! Those calves did not lead God's people out of Egypt; God led His people out of Egypt. Jeroboam led all the people in worship to the false gods.

Christ Connection: King Solomon failed to lead God's people perfectly. God's people needed a better king, a perfect king! Through David's family, God would send His own Son, Jesus Christ, to be a perfect King over God's people forever. Jesus brings His people together and leads them back to God.

Job
Job 1–42

MAIN POINT: JOB LEARNED THAT GOD IS ALL-POWERFUL, SOVEREIGN, AND GOOD.

Job was a wealthy man who loved God and wanted to follow God's plan. One day, Satan came before God.

"Job only follows You because You protect him and bless him," Satan said. "If You take away everything Job has, he will not follow You anymore."

So God gave Satan permission to take away everything Job had, but Satan was not allowed to hurt Job. Satan sent men to steal Job's animals. He caused Job's children to die. In one day, Job lost all of his wealth and his children. But Job continued to follow God.

Satan came to God again. He said, "If Job gets sick, he will not praise You anymore." So God gave Satan permission to make Job sick, but God did not let Satan kill Job. Job became ill with sores all over his skin.

Three of Job's friends came to visit Job. Job's friends did not comfort Job. They said, "Job, you must obey God. If you do what is right and stop sinning, God will give you back everything you lost."

"I haven't done anything wrong," Job said.

Finally, a man named Elihu came to speak to Job. "God is greater than man," Elihu explained. "God always does what is right."

Then God spoke to Job through a whirlwind. God helped Job understand that God is all-powerful, sovereign, and good. Job could not completely understand God's plans, but he could trust God. God is in control. Job was sorry for doubting God.

God gave back to Job everything he had lost—and much more!

Christ Connection: Job suffered and wanted a mediator—someone to bring him to God. This reminds us of Jesus, who suffered even though He had never sinned. Jesus is our Mediator. He suffered to pay the price for our sins and put an end to suffering on earth. Jesus brings us to God when we trust in Him.

Solomon Thought About Life
Ecclesiastes 1:1-11

MAIN POINT: LIFE HAS PURPOSE ONLY WITH GOD.

Solomon was the king of Israel. God gave Solomon wisdom, and Solomon shared his wisdom with others.

Solomon wrote down his thoughts about life, and we can read them in the Book of Ecclesiastes. These are some of the words King Solomon wrote.

"Apart from God, everything is meaningless. Nothing has meaning.

"Apart from God, does anyone have anything to show for their hard work? People are born, and then they die. Nothing lasts forever.

"Apart from God, everything is so tiring. We keep looking and we keep listening, but we are not satisfied." Only God truly satisfies.

"Apart from God, nothing on earth is new.

"Apart from God, no one remembers the people who were born long ago. And even the people who haven't been born yet will not be remembered by the people who are born after them."

Solomon thought about all of these things and he said, "God knows everything and will judge the good and the bad. Respect and obey God." This is what life is all about.

Christ Connection: Apart from God, life does not make sense. God created everything, and He gives everything a purpose. Jesus gives us purpose for living. Jesus came so that we might live for Him and have full, meaningful life. (John 10:10)

Praises of God's People
Psalms 1; 100; 110

MAIN POINT: PEOPLE WROTE SONGS TO PRAISE GOD BECAUSE OF WHO HE IS.

The Book of Psalms is a collection of songs written by many people over hundreds of years. Sometimes when God's people gathered, they sang psalms together to worship God.

Sometimes people wrote psalms when they were sad. Sometimes people wrote psalms to confess their sin to God and to ask for forgiveness.

The first psalm is about two ways to live: as a righteous person or as a wicked person. The two ways are like walking on two different paths. One path is dark and leads to death. The other path is bright and leads to life.

Psalm 100 is a song of thanks. God's people sang these words: "Give thanks to Him and praise His name. For Yahweh is good, and His love is eternal. His faithfulness will never end."

King David wrote Psalm 110. The psalm is about a king who is also a priest. David wrote that the Lord keeps His promises. He will be with the king and make him strong. He will give the king victory in the battle.

Christ Connection: In the Old Testament, whenever God's people cried out for mercy and forgiveness, praised God, or thanked Him, God heard their prayers. He promised to answer them, and He did, when He sent His Son, Jesus. Jesus meets our greatest need by providing salvation from sin so we can be forgiven and have eternal life.

THE GOSPEL
GOD'S PLAN for US

The gospel is the good news, the message about Christ, the kingdom of God, and salvation. Use these prompts to share the gospel with your kids.

GOD RULES. Ask: "Who is in charge at home?" Explain that because God created everything, He is in charge of everything. Read Revelation 4:11.

WE SINNED. Ask: "Have you ever done something wrong?" Tell kids that everyone sins, or disobeys God. Our sin separates us from God. Read Romans 3:23.

GOD PROVIDED. Explain that God is holy and must punish sin. God sent His Son, Jesus, to take the punishment we deserve. Read John 3:16.

JESUS GIVES. Ask: "What is the best gift you've ever received?" Say that Jesus took our punishment for sin by giving His life, and He gives us His righteousness. God sees us as if we lived the perfect life Jesus lived. This is the best gift ever! Read 2 Corinthians 5:21.

WE RESPOND. Explain that everyone has a choice to make. Ask: "Will you trust Jesus as your Savior and Lord? You can turn from self and sin and turn to Jesus." Read Romans 10:9-10.